T0194992

The
Rose
of Sharon

Sharon Byerly

WESTBOW
PRESS®
A DIVISION OF THOMAS NELSON
& ZONDERVAN

WestBow Press books may be ordered through booksellers or by contacting:

WestBow Press
A Division of Thomas Nelson & Zondervan
1663 Liberty Drive
Bloomington, IN 47403
www.westbowpress.com
1 (866) 928-1240

Interior Image Credit: Sharon Byerly

Scripture taken from the New King James Version®. Copyright © 1982 by Thomas Nelson. Used by permission. All rights reserved.

ISBN: 978-1-9736-3692-2 (sc)
ISBN: 978-1-9736-3694-6 (hc)
ISBN: 978-1-9736-3693-9 (e)

Library of Congress Control Number: 2018909734

Print information available on the last page.

WestBow Press rev. date: 8/16/2018

Introduction

My desire for these poems, which are a gift from God, and which I give back to Him as a ministry, is to see others come to Christ as a result of reading them; to see baby Christians desire to grow in their faith; to see others rooted, encouraged and uplifted in their Christian walk; and to see that all have a hunger for His Word.

I have been writing poetry since my adult son was a young boy (his poems are included in the "Family" section).

There is no "rhyme" or reason as to how God gives me His poems – to me anyway! I may get two or three in a day, a week or month, then none for a year or so. I've just learned He will give me a poem in His time, not when He is ready but when my spirit is ready to receive! I am quick to say God gets the glory for the poems I write because I don't think I could write two lines that rhyme without God giving me this awesome gift to share with you!

Contents

The Rose of Sharon

My name is Sharon, and my Rose is the Lord,
For without Him, I'm nothing but a bunch of thorns.
When I give myself to the Gardener to tend
I find He teaches me and is the best of friends.

He helps my spirit move past the lowly dirt and grass,
Past the thorns, and grow into blossoms unsurpassed.
You can have His love, too, if you haven't heard.
Have faith. Seek Him out by searching His Holy Word.

I can be lacking in love, selfish, stepping on people's toes,
But with His love teaching me, I'm blooming into a rose.
I accept His love and guidance and slowly begin to mend.
The old things slowly dissolve, and the old habits end.

He gives me good times to enjoy happily with ease,
And guides me through bad, so I learn how to please.
For it is through weakness that we learn to be strong,
And it is through pain that we can help others along.

I pray that my "Rose" you invite into your heart,
And that some of these words will help you start
To know and relish and rely on His mighty powers
To help you through all your good and bad hours.

I Died, He Lives

I died mentally when my mind totally gave out -- twice
So broken I might be a vegetable the rest of my life,
But Jesus ever lives to be the Great Physician for me,
He worked through twenty-seven ECT's, returning me to normalcy.

The doctor said basically I died after inhaling too much smoke,
Miracles, doctors, ambulance all tried my death to revoke,
But it's Jesus, who lives in me, who gave me back my life
To share with you that He is greater than any strife.

I die spiritually anytime I sin or disobey my Lord.
I feel guilty when I know I have gone against His Word,
But Jesus lives to ever make intercessions for my sins,
He forgives me and welcomes me back into the fold again.

How many ways can I die in need of His saving power?
It happens all the time; sometimes even hour by hour,
But Jesus loves me, saves me, and walks with me day after day.
I may die, but Jesus lives and showers me with love and grace.

MY FRIENDS

Birthdays

(All the little kids could not pronounce "Robert", thus it came out Rah-rah.)

Robert, I went high and low looking for a card.
But it turned out to be a job that was really hard.
There were cards for husbands, wives, daughters and sons,
Cards for girlfriends and boyfriends, but not the right ones.

There were cards that were feminine, with frills and flowers,
Cards with "icky" verses that would make you sick for hours!
I just couldn't seem to find a simple card that would say,
You know, "I hope you have a real 'Rah-rah' of a birthday!"

Goodbyes

(To a friend leaving work to start her own business, a maid service.)

Claire, how that old saying go?
"Parting is such sweet sorrow"?
That's how I feel about you today
For this place will be emptier with you away.

I'm happy you have a chance for new pursuits.
I know you'll be able to handle all the "recruits".
I'm sure you will do a real "thorough" job,
Make a real "clean sweep", be a hit with the "mop"!

We'll miss your bright face, your charming smile,
Your close friendship, matchless wit, and wile.
Please come and see us, if just once in a while.
You really don't have to put yourself in exile.

Friends should stay friends even when far away
'Cause you're close to our heart, and there you'll stay,
It will take time and effort before your business really zings,
But then call on us to celebrate with you, and we'll all sing.

Our Friend

The Lord is a mighty friend on whom you can depend,
He can certainly help you now to start to mend.
He's the only one who can help to fill the void.
We know, because He has given us peace and joy.

The secret is not in waiting on Him to do
But in asking Him to come in and help you.
It takes some action on our parts to get it started.
As He said, "Ask, seek, knock," and it shall be imparted.

It takes some time to get to know the Lord,
But isn't this true of any friend you adore?
We're just two friends who have experience and care,
And we're not afraid to tell you to try, to dare!

The goodness of His Spirit is something that's in you.
We know you have it because of all the things you do.

We're sure you've always had the Lord, just like we had Him, too.
But, before, we never really sought His will in everything we do.

What a blessing it would be for Him to work in you
'Cause not all Christians have the sweetness that you do.

Love,

Sharon and Judy

Marriage God's Way

Satan is attacking us from all around,
To keep us and our marriage from being sound.
God's plan is for husband and wife to be one,
But the devil will try every ploy under the sun.

God's plan is oneness--mind, body, Spirit, and soul--
An intimate relationship to keep us whole.
God's authority is first, and then the husband over the wife,
This hierarchy produces order and lessens strife.

The closer we get to living God's perfect plan,
The more firm against the devil we have to stand.
He may attack the woman, the weaker vessel, first,
So protect your wife from spiritual hunger and thirst.

Pray earnestly, and put on the whole armor of God,
Read His Word daily to help you on the path you trod,
Husband, love your wife, and wife, submit to him,
And do not allow the devil a chance to get in.

Ask God to guide your steps together down one path of life,
Sharing life's joy and blessings, enduring and growing through strife.
Husband, as her spiritual leader, love her as Christ loves you,
Wife, give your husband reverence and honor in all you do.

Divorce

In the midst of worry, argument, and strife,
You cannot get a person to try to change his life.
That person is not worried about changing self and being good,
But is focusing, out of defense, on what's wrong with your mood.

You said you'd never have left if he'd said he would change,
But were you willing to do the same for the sake of his name?
Sometimes it is only by becoming the wife that to him appeals
That we instill the desire for that person to reach up to his ideals.

You have to be able to forgive all past faults, sins, and paid dues,
Because that is what the Lord has done for him and for you.
I know that is a weak spot for you especially to accept,
And that is why it is so important for you to forgive his debts.

I wish you could realize how much I wish to help in these things.
I have given myself to the Lord and feel the victory He brings.
Even if you feel the other person has been much more at fault,
If you start with yourself, you'll see miracles very soon start!

Wedding Wish

May these sheets remind you as you greet each new day
To try to be in love with each other in every way.

May these sheets remind you at night as you go to bed
To take care of any arguments before you lay down your heads.

May they bless your life together as you go along
And help to keep in your hearts a bright and happy song.

May they remind you of your joys and help to forget any sorrow.
May they remind you to forget yesterday and remember tomorrow.

An Award

Congratulations, Vicki, no one deserves this honor more than you
For when the chips were down, you chose to rise above and come through.
You have worked so hard and deserve all the accolades we can extend,
But especially since you have had personal trials with which to contend.

You are a person we all can truly admire
You have set an example to which we all can aspire
You know that we really are so very proud
You certainly deserve to rest on this cloud.

We hope that the trip is the chance you've been looking for
To get away, to relax, have a good time, and open new doors.
It's always nice to get away for a little spell,
You need it, you deserve it, and we wish you well.

If I had this morning just a little more time,
I'd make this a much longer verse and rhyme
For you deserve as much praise as I can write,
From the bottom of my heart, I'm glad you're in the light.

Thank You

When the chips are down
And it seems like bad times abound,
It's certainly a thrill to have found
That it's nice to have good friends around.

Trials put everyone to the test,
But I feel so extremely blessed,
And if by now you haven't guessed,
It's because of you and all the rest.

Thank you for your love and care,
Thank you for your many prayers,
Thank you for being much more than fair,
Thank you for friendships cherished and rare!

Nothing could help us better through our trials
Than all of you who offer your concern and smiles.
This road we travel is full of some pretty rough miles,
But with friends like you, it's certainly worthwhile!

Good Luck, President Reagan

We were tired of high prices and double-digit inflation,
And all the many ills affecting our beloved nation,
So we made our choice, loud and clear, by electing you.
We pledge our support, and ask God's help in all that you do.

Ask the Lord to be your adviser before you speak a word or do a deed
For He is the most important confidante you could ever heed.
Please remember that our prayers are with you each and every day.
Your leadership is in God's hands, so listen to Him along the way.

May He grant you good health so that your leadership will be strong.
May He give you wisdom to make the decisions to keep us rolling along.
May He give you compassion to help the people's cares and hunger cease.
But most of all, may He give you love to help keep the world at peace.

For any man, the job you hold is a very awesome task.
But without the Lord, it's more than anyone could ask.
To make the decisions that are right, good, and true,
The Lord needs to be able to lead, guide, and direct you.

MY FAMILY

Dad

Happy Birthday to you, Dad
You're the best any girl ever had.
Thanks for picking me up when I fell,
Thanks for helping me be strong and well.

Thanks for your strict discipline in my youth
Even though then I thought it very uncouth!
Thanks for giving me a faith to get me through,
A love for Jesus to teach me to be true.

I hope that as you reach fifty-five
You find many reasons for being alive.
I hope you have a very nice birthday,
"I love You" is what I most want to say!

Happy Mother's Day

I've been noticing that your life has changed much,
And I know it's a result of Jesus' tender touch.
You've always been a nice person, mother, and friend,
But now I see more love, more care, your life more content.

The Seminar that changed your life has changed mine also.
I thought you too persistent then, but thanks for not letting go.
You know that by keeping at me to go to that meeting
You helped save me and received in Heaven special seating.

If you'd like to know why I feel this way, really,
Please read James, Chapter 5, Verses 19 and 20.
You've helped restore me from the error of my ways; you see
The Seminar was the turning point in letting Jesus <u>live</u> in me.

I love you and appreciate your care, help and support,
And enjoy your friendship and progress in the Lord.
I've wanted you to know and to tell you in this way,
You're great and I wish you a Happy Mother's Day!

Happy Mother's Day

In thinking about Mother's Day and your being so kind,
Some fond memories surface and come to mind.
Even though embarrassed to go to Cohen's to be dressed,
I appreciate that it kept us clothed and you less stressed!

Homemade ice cream (especially cherry nut) all flavors were good,
Brownies, cookies, upside down cake, were all great tasting food.
Parties with hors d'oeu'vres, special sandwiches minus the crust,
All made today's bland and instant tasteless food a real bust.

Meatloaf, tuna casseroles, spaghetti and roast beef,
Simple dishes made with love and wonderful to eat.
I don't remember your actually "teaching" us to cook,
But by the best way--letting us hang around and look.

Except for ironing, how I disliked all the household chores,
Like vacuuming, dusting, bathrooms and mopping floors.
I know why I can take care of my home now,
Because you made sure my skills were really wow!

I thank God for my Mom who is witty and fun,
Who cares about others and whose trust has been won.
Thank you for your example, sacrifices and love,
But most of all, for pointing us to our Jesus up above!

Happy Anniversary, Mom & Dad

In a day when they say families are becoming extinct,
And that most couple's marriages are on the brink.
It's exciting to me to see you celebrating this
Thirty-four years of commitment to bliss.

We know that bliss is not always the state,
But you're commended for trying and making it rate
Among the steady marriages of your time and era
By sharing and caring and loving and staying together.

Thanks for showing us a marriage that's good,
That's an excellent example for the whole neighborhood.
We know that your love and faith is the basis for length
And this knowledge gives us and others much strength.

I thank the Lord for parents like you, for your care and love,
And for staying together through all times with help from above.
I ask the Lord to give you many more years to live prosperously,
And we wish you a very, very Happy 34th Wedding Anniversary!

Our Son, Ricky

August 18, 1977 – First Birthday

My Son, My Son
Oh how much you've grown.
In just one year
So many seeds you've sown.

You're happy, healthy, brave and shy
Sometimes you're mad, sometimes you cry.
But always you are seeking to know
How all the world around you grows.

And the seed that you have planted best
Will always stand time's test:

That's all the love and joy you've given us!

February, 1979 – Ricky, Age 2-1/2

Now you're two-and-a-half years old,
And you're really just as good as gold.
You've finally mastered the potty chair
And your "ABC's" with definite flair.

You can sing "Twinkle Twinkle Little Star",
You'd even like to drive my car!
You're already good at washing a dish,
And even making your bed if you wish.

You're in the stage of "Why", "How Come", "What For",
And now you can even reach the handles on the door.
You like to watch "Spiderman" and "Mork & Mindy"
And run and play outside, even if it's windy.

You're very adept at the spoken word,
Your manners and your prayers to the Lord.
You're really quite a fascinating Lad,
And we love you very much ...

Mom and Dad.

August 18, 1979 – Ricky, Age 3

Happy third birthday, Little Ricky.
You're cute and fun and really tricky.
You're not a baby anymore,
A big boy trying to learn the score.

There's lots of love in your little heart,
And love is always the most important part.
May Jesus show you how to love the best,
For your love for others is the supreme test.

It's hard to be so grown up at three.
You're just as smart as you can be.
You're fast, you're active, helpful, too.
You like to play and laugh and even boo-hoo!

You're race car bed is your pride and joy,
Ricky, isn't it fun to be a boy!
You're learning to do things by yourself,
It's fun, it's scary, but we'll always help.

We hope you have a nice birthday today
With cake, candy and friends along the way.
It's nice to see you growing so strong.
Remember, Mom and Dad are here to help you along.

August 18, 1980 – Ricky, Age 4

It's really just amazing to me and Dad
That four is the birthday you're now at.
We know that's not old enough to you
because we know you'd like to be 10 or 22!

Son, we know that to you those ages look great,
But we'd like for you to enjoy <u>each</u> year you make.
There's something wonderful about each day,
So enjoy it now before it slips away.

When you are ten you can ride a bike,
And when you're 22 you can wed a wife!
But today you're a wonderful four years young
And we love to see you play, learn and have fun.

We do realize that you're pretty "old" for your years,
And we will let you do lots of things as you mature.
So just have fun, relax, and be a boy today; and hey,
Remember to keep trusting your parents along the way.

The "Stranger"

Luke 24:13-36

I was grieving over the loss of closeness with a friend
When my Lord, my best friend, kindly stepped in.
He said, "Sharon, remember the story of two disciples, sadly
Walking down the road after my death, grieving for me".

"They did not recognize me as their friend as I explained
How I had to suffer and die before coming again.
As I finished talking and we reached their home,
I would not have invited myself in, but would have gone on."

I listened and heard that I should be a friend
Who cares, listens, loves and helps to mend.
But I should not force my love, like You didn't on the pair,
So, I can be available to anyone who needs my love and care.

Lord, help me to be the loving kind of Christian
That your two disciples were way back then.
Even though they were grieving for You, their crucified Lord,
They asked You, the "Stranger", to share their room and board.

MY ROSE, THE LORD

God's Word

Don't make the mistake of many a poor soul
Who won't read God's Word in part or in whole.
It is our Life's Manual from God to each self,
And it does no good for us sitting upon a shelf.

The Bible is the number #1 seller ever written down.
Too bad it's not the number #1 read in every town.
His amazing Word is His love letter just for your eyes.
How long will you wait to open it, to discover, to realize?

The Psalms He wrote for David to melt his heart
Were also for you to reach the depths of your inward parts.
The Letters he wrote through Paul to show how to live
Are just as appropriate for anyone today who desires to give.

Don't come up to your last day on this earth
Without reading His Book of infinite worth.
Accept Jesus today as your personal Savior and Lord.
Ask Him to help you daily to read and understand His Word.

No one knows how long they have before they may be gone,
So make your choice for Jesus and your eternity a song.
Spend what time you have left in this strange, alien place,
Developing your friendship with Jesus by seeking His face.

B lessed
I nstruction
B y the
L ord
E ternal

When to Read the Bible

If you're not a Christian, reading the Bible won't do much for you,
A veil covers your mind and the true meaning doesn't come through.
Only after you accept Jesus as your Savior and Lord and pick up the Book,
Will the veil fall away as you read and study; then you will get a clear look.

II Corinthians 3:14

God's Veil

2Co 3:13 - unlike Moses, *who* put a veil over his face so that the children
of Israel could not look steadily at the end of what was passing
away.
2Co 3:14 - But their minds were blinded. For until this day the same veil
remains unlifted in the reading of the Old Testament, because
the *veil* is taken away in Christ
2Co 3:15 - But even to this day, when Moses is read, a veil lies on their
heart.
2Co 3:16 - Nevertheless when one turns to the Lord, the veil is taken away.

The Word of God is understood with the Mind of Christ.
You can only have His Mind if you invite Him in your life,
Then the veil is lifted as you study His Word and heed.
Then His Spirit will help you understand what you need.

As you commit to daily study God's Word in prayer,
He will listen and guide you and answer your every care.
He will answer you personally through His Scripture choice.
What an awesome privilege to hear His still, quiet voice!

So come before His presence in worship and praise.
Be thankful that He loves you; wants you to know His ways.
God really wants you to know Him and the glory of His grace.
You are just as important to Him as any member of the human race.

So please remember that the only way you can come in to Him
Is to recognize your fallen state and repent of all your sins.
Then accept Jesus as personal Savior of your eternal soul.
Trust Him by His Holy Spirit to make you righteous and whole.

So let Sweet Jesus remove the Veil from your heart and eyes.
Your understanding will be enlarged and your mind surprised.
As you spend more time in God's Word learning His ways,
He will walk with you and reveal His way all of your days!

Battle of Flowers
(The Parade Sniper)

You lifted me up and carried me away
On that fearful, frightening, momentous day.
You sharpened my senses and made me realize
That danger was lurking there before my eyes.

I heard a shot, someone thought to start the parade,
But I caught the eye of the Cop as he turned and swayed.
I saw his surprise, his shock, and his dread,
And felt Your presence as I grabbed my son and fled.

I felt a sharp pain in my leg as I ran away,
And worried where my friend was in this terrible melee.
I made it to safety to my friend's office next door,
My friend was there, wounded, but safe as before.

We stopped and thanked You for sparing us in this plight,
And I noticed my friend started to see if others were all right.
I learned that You help and all things turn out for our good,
And I'm sorry I wasn't braver, and hoped next time I would.

You see, if I am trusting myself solely to the Lord
Then I must know that He'll guide me safely through any storm,
And that should leave me free to help others in their strife
To show Your love and power, even at the risk of my own life.

God-Love

His love is a many-splendored thing.
It makes souls chime and hearts ring.
The secret to a heart is His love there,
And God's love is something we all can share.

We can let someone know that we understand his care
Either because we know or because we have been there.
That's one reason Jesus came to earth, you know,
To share our cares, our joys, our sorrow, our woe.

There are many ways to show God's love to those we meet
By a kind word, an understanding ear or a look so sweet,
By willingness to do things asked of us with cheerful deed,
But also a kind offering to help when we see someone in need.

God is a person never far away,
When we practice His love day to day.
He understands what we're going through,
But most of all He <u>wants</u> to help us, too.

Help Me Tell Others

Thank you, Lord, for blessing my day
For lighting my path, showing me the way.
I ask that you bless all my friends, too.
Show them how wonderful it is to trust in You.

Help me to show them that Your love is true.
Help me to aid them when they're looking for You.
By my words and actions let me always say,
You are my Savior and I trust You always.

Sometimes it's hard to know who needs to hear,
But Your Spirit aids me in guiding my ear
To discern when a soul is in some kind of need,
That Your Word is what they most want to heed.

Allow me to be Your vessel to lead them toward
The peace, beauty and truth of Your Everlasting Word.
Let Your Words speak truly always through me
To show whomever I meet how you care and want them to be.

Letting Go

Lord, You wish me to give You all my worries, all my cares.
I know I can do it, but it's hard even <u>knowing</u> You're there.
I will relinquish my doubts, my cares, worries and woes,
For I know You want to take care of me wherever I may go.

Help Your Light shine through me to all whom I may meet,
Be it family, friends or even the stranger on the street.
I think this is why You want me to give you all my strife
So that I am free to be a good friend, Christian and wife.

I know it's hard when I'm feeling pain, sorrow and grief,
But this is exactly the time You are ready to give relief.
I feel Your strength within giving peace of mind and heart,
And making it easier to make each day a fresh, new start.

Help me to follow You, to grow strong, and never to go astray,
Because no matter what happens, I know Yours is the only Way.
Help me never to question the things that happen to me or why.
I know <u>my</u> best interest is at <u>Your</u> heart even though I may die.

9/11 Day of Prayer

Seventeen years ago our towers fell,
And today we pray for our nation as well.
Today is a National Call to Repentance and Prayer.
Is anybody aware and does anyone care?

Are we aware that we're a nation fallen in sin?
Do we see that we are crumbling from within?
Do we know the foundations are breaking apart,
And that most of all we're breaking God's heart?

This nation was founded by God-believing men
Who put their lives, families and faith in Him.
As long as we kept that trust, God kept us secure,
A "shining city on a hill", one which did endure.

All the world looked to us, they copied us, sang our songs.
They came to our shores however they could, in teeming throngs.
But our success is because we have given glory to God,
And let His light shine out from us on the path that we trod.

If we now desert Him from being our God and our Lord,
He will no longer hold back His terrible swift sword.
But be assured that He loves us and for this Jesus was sent.
He's patiently waiting for us to admit our sins and repent!

So please use this time before your Maker to search your soul,
Repent of your own sins and allow Him to make you whole,
Then pray for others, our leaders and the sins of our nation,
And maybe we will receive mercy from the God of all creation!

My Lord's Prayer

Our Father who art in Heaven
Who saves us from sin's leaven

Hallowed be Thy Name,
Father, Lord, God, Jehovah, all Holy and the same

Thy Kingdom come,
Where we are waiting like Jesus to become

Thy Will be done,
Through the Spirit and Jesus Your Son

On earth as it is in Heaven,
With righteousness, peace, and no sin

Give us this day our daily bread.
It will always stand us in good stead

And forgive us our sins,
We have such a plethora; great against us are the loud dins

As we forgive those who trespass against us.
How can we not forgive when You have forgiven—we must!

And lead us not into temptation.
We fall into it so easily on our own volition

But deliver us from evil,
And all the coming worldly upheaval

For Thine is the kingdom, the power and the glory.
It is all about You, Father, Jesus, Holy Spirit: Your Story.

Forever
And ever, and ever, and ever
Amen
Amen and Amen

My Shepherd

The Lord is my Shepherd, I shall not want,
    He is my guide and provides all I need.
He makes me to lie down in green pastures
    providing rest and physical food.
He leads beside the still waters
    providing calm and refreshing drink.
He restores my soul
    providing peace in my spirit.
He leads in paths of righteousness for His Name's sake,
    with a peaceful spirit, I am open to His leading.
Even though I walk in the valley of the shadow of death,
I will fear no evil for Thou art with me.
    How can I fear shadow or substance when You are here.
Your rod and staff they comfort me,
    I know You use them to guide and direct me.
You prepare a table for me in the presence of my enemies.
    If you prepare it then I know you are there to protect me.
You anoint my head with oil, my cup runneth over.
    You give me Your Holy Spirit and blessings without limit.
Surely goodness and mercy will follow me all the days of my life.
    Your blessings will follow me all the days of my earthly life,
And I will dwell in the house of the Lord forever,
    And I will dwell in Your house for eternity!

What a Great Good Shepherd!

Praise to the Lord

Today is a day to give thanks to the Lord
For all the good things in life He affords.
Let today's thanks be the start of a new way
In which we thank Him for our blessings every day.

Sure we have problems, some worries and cares,
But there's always something to show us He's there:
Be it a beautiful sunshiny day, or a close and special friend,
Or blessings fallen our way, His love shows up again and again.

Today we give thanks for our friends and our family
For being able to show love and to live happily.
We are thankful for the love You give us to share,
And for sending Jesus down to us from His home up there.

Tomorrow we give thanks for another new beginning,
A day to start fresh, smiling, always winning,
A day to entrust our lives to the Lord,
To thank Him for the many blessings He affords.

Giving Thanks

T hanking God for His Love and

H is Son Jesus in Heaven above and for

A ll His Blessings bestowed on His creatures below

N ow gathered to thank Him one by one.

K nowing we have many blessings we can name,

S urely we can recall a few to count.

G iving God credit as in praise we mount

I n search of His glory, honor and praise,

V oicing our thanks in love we raise

I n tune with one another in sweet accord

N otes of thankful giving lifted to Him heavenward.

G od hears our praise and thanks with His thankful heart.

Forgiveness

Oh, Lord, give me a heart of forgiveness for those who sin against me,
For my manifold, many, millions of sins are what put You on the Tree.
If I say "I forgive" 70x7 times to one person even for the same sin,
Doesn't that mean I'm being bitter and resentful and haven't forgiven?

Or, maybe it means that I <u>have</u> forgiven and the enemy is just being unkind
In keeping me off track and distracted so my focus is not on Christ's mind.
So when I think of a situation over and over that's already been confessed,
I should just give it to Jesus and know that it's been lovingly addressed.

If I choose to forgive someone his sin from my heart,
Then I have already really desired to do my part.
It's because I desire that there be no rift between me and You,
That I desire to forgive others so that I can be true.

Somehow that sounds selfish but it is what Your Prayer says to do,
That I must forgive others or You cannot forgive my sins, too.
It's a complicated thing to comprehend and accomplish.
Please give me Your heart to obey You in this command and wish.

Freedom

He has made my burden easy, my path light,
So I am free to follow His will and do what's right.
Even if I am free of being naturally selfish,
I realize it takes a lot for God to make me righteous.

I freely choose and desire to do His will in my life.
His Spirit is what makes it possible with less strife,
For I know that I still have my sinful nature within,
But His power overrides and helps me to overcome sin.

The Lord is with me when I wish to be with Him,
And when I seek Him, He always lets me in.
No good thing of the Lord's will be withheld from me
When I freely choose to live and walk uprightly...

Thank God I'm Free!!

Jesus Knew

You suffered pain and torture as You died upon that tree.
Maybe worse for You was that you knew Before that it had to be.
From time eternity You knew You would have to die for me.
How terrible to know beforehand the pain and suffering You would see.

To know ahead of time that You would feel the thorns upon Your brow.
To experience the beatings in your thoughts seems worse somehow,
But You went through all this to save us from all our sins, all our loss.
Perhaps seeing the <u>end</u> result is also what kept You going to the Cross.

You reminded Your followers that long ago Your death was prophesied,
That the Temple would be destroyed and in three days rebuilt on that site.
You taught the Disciples that You must be killed, then be raised to the light.
You told them more than once but still unbelieving they stayed behind.

So distraught in the Garden, You knew exactly what it meant to obey,
Saying "the Spirit is willing; the flesh is weak" it was difficult to pray.
You agreed with God's plan, but your flesh was horrifically tempted to stay.
You finished praying knowing Your time had come and what was to be that day.

You had seen your death mentally and knew physically what it meant for You,
Yet You went to the Cross inflicted with suffering and shame that was <u>our</u> due.
You already knew what would happen as You walked the hill to Calvary.
You went to save us, because You loved us, even though You knew…

… and You went anyway!

Jesus Knew

Y
O
U

W
You knew You werE God's Sacrificial Lamb
N
T

A
N
Y
W
A
Y

How would you and I react if we knew we were going to die,
Not just going to die; but also how and when all of our life.
Could we handle life with grace, joy, and love like Christ?
(Maybe that's why God doesn't let us know ahead of time.
Mt. 16:21, 17:22-23, 20:18-19, 26:2, 26:36-42, Ecc. 3:2)

Death's Mystery

Most of us have this fear of death that seems to be innate.
Perhaps it's there to remind us to seek God before it's too late,
But God, our Father, does not want us to worry, fret, or fear,
Especially about giving up this last step of our life so dear.

Several times in His Word He compares death to sleep.
What can be painful about falling into dreamy sleep so deep,
Just to close your eyes one last time and leave behind your care,
No more pain, no sorrow, and when you wake Jesus is there.

Now that's if you believe in Jesus you will awake with Him,
But if you don't believe in Jesus you will awake in your sin.
You will sleep in death and you will awake again,
But you will live for eternity in shame and contempt.   Daniel 12:2

Now the choice is yours; it always has been,
But Jesus is the only answer to pay for your sin.
If you choose any other way that you think Heaven might gain,
Then why in the world would God sacrifice Jesus for your pain.

So God's Word says that ALL will die and live in some eternal space.
It just depends on you and where you choose to make your place.
God has made the initial choice easy in that there are only TWO PATHS:
Believe in Jesus' payment for your sins or take another and feel God's wrath!

The Last Frontier

O, Death where is your victory, where your Sting
For death is swallowed up when in Jesus we sing.
Perhaps we are most afraid of the mystery of death
Because no one can tell us how to cope with this step.

That is, no one but Jesus, who has showed us, as in other things,
For He has tasted death for us, showed us how to conquer the stings,
And we have proof from Him of the Victory on the other side
From His death and resurrection into God's heavenly life.

There are many kinds of death besides the physical that we fear,
But Jesus is the answer to the other kinds that cripple and adhere.
He can wake us from the awful death of our old sinful spirit,
Help us shake off dead emotions and live gloriously without limit.

Jesus has said to store our treasures in Heaven
Where they cannot rust or decay and cannot be taken,
So when death strikes one we love and takes him away,
Think of him as "Heavenly Treasure" who'll welcome you on your day.

Jesus will help to lead us through the last frontier, the gate of death.
He has <u>promised</u> His presence to go with us and give us rest.
No good thing will He withhold from them that walk uprightly,
Including the promise of life beyond death and that for eternity.

If Only You Will Believe

Jesus knew He would suffer crucifixion – a terrible ordeal.
He also knew he'd rise victorious, His victory would be real.
Even though they sealed His tomb with a heavy permanent seal,
The soldiers said Jesus' body was stolen and gave a lying spiel.

But Jesus was raised on Sunday taking the women's breath away.
Indeed He held the whole world in His hands that momentous day.
The Father's plan set up in ages past was that day totally finished.
Everything Jesus did was in no way, by no one, at all diminished.

The women came to the tomb, saw Jesus alive and believed.
Peter and John ran to the tomb and deduced and perceived,
But the rest of the Disciples questioned, doubted, and did not go,
Even though He had predicted these things and kept them in the know.

Jesus did not wait around for His Disciples to come to Him,
He met with them, even walked through walls so they would feel forgiven,
He ate with them, let Thomas touch the nail-scarred hands He'd been given.
He talked, walked, spoke, and taught them before He left for Heaven.

If you're like the Disciples who were disbelieving, doubting, full of pride,
But finally believed after seeing Jesus 40 days and over 500 people beside,
Then they saw Him rise in the sky right before their very eyes,
Then these true words Jesus sent for you to believe for your faith and guide.

Matthew 28:1-2, 28:13-15, 28:17
Luke 24:27
John 20:30-31, Acts 1:2-9

Rewards

The yearning in our hearts for the perfect love, the perfect place
Was placed there by the Lord to urge us to seek His face.
He is the only one who can give security and really please us,
And He has given us the way through His virgin-born Son, Jesus.

Maybe the yearning in our hearts You've brought us to bear
As proof that You have the perfect world waiting up there.
When as many as can and will have called upon Your name,
Then You will fulfill our yearnings without any blame.

Help us to remember perfection cannot be fulfilled here,
But we start in the hope we will achieve the reward sometime near,
And with the help of Jesus we can certainly now begin
Because we know You have planned for us the perfect end.

A beautiful heaven where there are no more tears,
An eternal amount of happy times and abundant years,
A place where there is joy, singing, abounding grace,
And for you, me, all of us, He'll prepare a special place.

Easter Morn

Today we celebrate our risen Lord
The promise as fulfilled in His Word
Today is His glorious Easter morn
When things are new, not old and worn.

Today we give thanks for His life,
For His death, and after His strife,
For His resurrected body and soul
And for rebirth making us whole.

We thank You on this Easter Morn for making Jesus live again
And also for making each of us new, glorified, and reborn in Him.
The biggest miracle of Jesus resurrected life and His supreme glory
Is the new beginning in spirit for each of us – the "Old, Old Story"

We appreciate this gift from You
And want to feel it each day anew.
It belongs to all, but is so rare,
Let us remember this gift to share.

Jesus loved You and us so very much
That we should always keep in touch
With the power and mystery of His gift
And pass it to others to help uplift.

Today is Easter but it could also be
The Day of New Birth when you really see
Jesus died for your sins to set you apart,
If you repent and ask Him into your heart.

If all the world could share this day
Inside their souls in this special way
Your mission on earth would be done,
Victory in Jesus would be <u>totally</u> won!

Jesus Prays For Me

When I'm down and don't seem to have a prayer
That is exactly the time that Jesus is there.
When life gets hard and seems really rough,
Jesus shows me that His grace is quite enough.

When I get to a point, it seems, of no return
That is when Jesus says, "Now, you can learn."
When I say, "Lord, I just can't handle this."
He says, "I will bring you up out of the abyss."

When my sins and darkness get me down,
That's when Jesus let's me know He's around.
When distractions try their best to intrude,
That is when Jesus gives me a quiet interlude.

When I feel that no one knows my care,
That is when Jesus shows me His comfort rare.
When I feel unloved, afraid, and alone,
That is when Jesus shows me I am His own.

When I remember to praise Him in all things
Oh, the peace and love and joy He brings.
When I can say "thank you" even for my trials,
He works all things for good and restores the smiles.

In Your Presence

My Lord is with me wherever I go,
He will never leave or forsake me, that I know.   Heb. 13:6
He has assured me of His presence in His Word,
And I feel Him with me at all times, bad or good.

When I open the door of my heart and invite Him in
He will come in and dine with me and I with Him.   Rev. 3:20
I may at times in my life stray or wander from His love,
But He can never deny His love, it's anchored from above.

When I may feel sad, far off, or estranged from God,
I need to think about a wrong turn I've made on the path I trod.
If I ever tend to wonder "Where is God in this part?"   Ps. 46:1
I need to say, "God is <u>here</u>; where is <u>my</u> mind and heart?"

God has promised to go with us from Bible stories of old,
And grace can't be found unless You go with us as Moses told. Gen. 43:14-17
Now Jesus has entered Heaven once to put away sin   Heb. 9:24-28
For us, and now we await His coming, for eternity, again.

Then we will truly be in His presence for all eternity.
Even now He is preparing our Eternal Home and City.
He has promised that He will come again to receive us,
So that where He is, we will be with Him, that's a promise!   John 14:1-6

Don't Side-Step Your Ladder!

God promises, and He provides, a ladder going from Heaven to earth,
To help in every circumstance, in life, in death, and even in birth.
He sends His ministering angels to travel up and down the stairs.
They help each and every one of us in all of our many affairs.

In anything we have to carry, any burden, whether heavy or light,
Our God desires to show the path which He alone has made just right.
He will provide His heavenly stairs, and He alone can show the way,
But He leaves to us the task of listening for what He is going to say.

God may not speak in loud clear tones, or voice easy to discern,
But He asks our dedicated time, in order to listen, seek, and learn.
So He may tell you softly, quietly, "Child, I have your ladder here."
But, if you are not listening closely, then the steps may disappear.

God's gracious love may provide a second Ladder, second time,
But you should know the first was quicker, and much easier to climb.
Be fully aware that our God speaks, but in His own mysterious way.
Don't side-step your Ladder, thinking "I don't believe what God may say."

My ladder was to write this poem and share with you my life.
I side-stepped it by thinking, "This can't be, I am used to strife."
God speaks not only in reproof, but often in love, mercy, and grace.
JESUS IS THE LADDER God came down to save the human race!

Angels Proclamations

God's angels on high come down to Earth to proclaim good news.
They are His messengers doing His Will and expressing His views.
Throughout the Old and New Testament they come to our aid,
To let us know that God is for us and not to be anxious or afraid.

When Daniel prayed and continued to pray and prayed again,
The Angel finally came and said he had been delayed by Satan.
But he let Daniel know that his prayer had been heard on high,
Since the very first moment he had uttered a deep, mournful sigh.

As Zacharias was accomplishing his Temple lot and course,
A Holy Angel appeared startling and scaring him completely hoarse.
The angel proclaimed that he and Elizabeth would have a baby son,
And would name him John; Zacharias was struck dumb, stunned.

The Shepherds were taking care of their flocks by night
When Angels appeared proclaiming a supernatural sight.
They led the Shepherds to a humble Bethlehem stall,
And sang in heavenly chorus that was heard by one and all!

Angels have always been proclaimers of good news and bad,
Messengers of God's Will whether the news is happy or sad.
Best news they proclaim is Jesus Christ' Good News--the Gospel.
Now we are proclaimers to others of this News, all fear to dispel!

It does not take a fearful Angel to enlighten you to the News,
And it doesn't have to be a supernatural Angel to express God's views.
Today He has other Christians who can testify to Jesus' presence,
And there is always the testimony of His Written Word, His Essence.

"Christ"mas

This Christmas Day is a very wonderful, special holy day.
Help us to remember to celebrate it in just this way,
For Christmas was the day of our Lord Jesus' humble birth
To show God's love and to save a fallen, sinful Mother Earth.

Let us not only celebrate His human birth so many, many years ago,
But also His birth in our spirit which renews and makes us know
That it is by letting the spirit of the Christ live in and through us,
That we are made whole, acceptable "Children of Light" from lowly dust.

When Jesus was born onto this earth, God put all His love into His Son
To show us His Love, the way to live and how the Victory could be won.
For through Adam we're all made sinners and have fallen from God's grace,
But through accepting the perfect love of His Son we too can win the race.

Perhaps we should not celebrate the birth of God's Son on Christmas Day,
Without also remembering that His death was to show us in the same way,
The unending love of the Father who loves us so much that He not only gave,
But allowed His Son to live, teach, heal, and also to die in order to save.

There are many wonderful things to be thankful for on this Christmas Day:
The wonderful, saving, merciful love, and grace of God that is with us always.
He has given us salvation and eternal life if we only have faith in His Son.
He forgives our sins, picks us up when we fall, and makes us whole and One.

Merry Christmas

Today we celebrate Your virgin birth,
Your arrival on Your own created earth.   John 1:1-4
The globe You lovingly created from time immemorial,
You now temporarily exchange from heaven eternal.

Shepherds saw the star and knelt in Your praise,   Luke 2:15
On that beautiful, glorious, day of days.
They knew that there was no other like it ever,
The day their King was born to reign forever.

Angels had waited to praise God for this eons long,   Luke:2-13-14
To break into Glorias on just this particular song.
Now Heaven could no longer hold back their praise,
For the Baby Jesus, Wonderful Counselor, Prince of Peace.

King Herod rejected the Babe, even killed all under two,   Matt. 2:16
Just to try to get rid of all possible threats from the Jews.
But, three Wise Men traveled hundreds of miles on that day,
Bringing three special gifts to prepare Him on His way.

Let us not be like Herod who pretended to worship Jesus,
By decorating trees, eating, but denying His presence in us.
If you give gifts but have not received the gift of eternal life from Christ,
You are only celebrating a shallow, worldly Christmas...   John 3:16

Jesus really is the reason for the Season!

Christmas Gifts

If it's only gifts with bows that are pretty and neat,
Presents to open or toys, books and sweets.
If it is only gathering with those we only had time to tweet,
And sitting together at the table to share a meal and eat.

Then, that's not only Christmas, not the real reason Christ came.
He was born because He loved us and was willing to share our pain.
He came to show He loved us and share in our lives at His birth.
He came to give not physical gifts but the gift of Himself to suffering earth.

So let us put Christ back in Christmas when we give gifts this year.
Wrap them in the love of Jesus and tie them up with Godly cheer.
Jesus was born as a baby because He loved us with all His heart,
And He died on the Cross because He saved us His eternal life to impart.

God says there is only one way to receive the gift of eternal life,
And that is by believing in His Son, Jesus Christ, and His sacrifice.
If there were any other way in heaven or earth to pay for our sins,   John 3:16
God certainly would have spared His only Son and let us enter in.

This Christmas gift is free because God loves us with all that He has,
But it cost Him more to give it to us than we could possible realize.
This is God's plan which we may not easily understand or fathom,
But it's <u>His</u> Plan, only <u>one</u> way, because Jesus paid our <u>entire ransom</u>!

On Your Wedding Day and Beyond

May you love one another not for your packaging but your content,
Not just loving when you feel like it but for your vowed intent.
For love is not just made up of a feeling, an action or a word,
But on the promise you make together today before your Lord.

It will be, at times, an impossible thing for you to do,
To love one another as Jesus has first loved you.
But when impossibility rears its ugly head,
Jesus is always there to love and work in your stead.

Make Jesus your primary focus and your first concern,
Things will not get as blurred when from Him you learn.
Spend time in prayer and study with the Lord each day,
And you will be more prepared to be open to His way.

Husband, love your wife, for this is right with God.
Show her that she is important on the path you trod.
Wife, respect your husband and submit to him in all things.
It's God's plan and with His help you'll see the joy it brings.

Ephesians 5:33

Choices

A child learns rebellion from observing an unsubmissive wife,
by seeing how she argues with her husband and tries to control his life.
Will you allow your children to see a wife who reverences her man,
or a woman who argues, disagrees and controls as much as she can?

Your childrens' image of their Father in Heaven above,
is based on their life with their father here and his love.
Will you allow them to see a glimpse of a loving, forgiving Dad,
or someone who leaves them, is selfish, and makes them sad?

A husband loves a woman who anticipates and meets his needs,
who submits to his authority and every word she hears and heeds.
Will you put your husband's wants and needs ahead of yourself,
or think only of yours and treat him like a dusty book on a shelf?

A wife loves a man to be the spiritual leader of the home,
who will grow and pray and study with her and never roam.
Will you rule over your wife and children with God's tender, loving care,
or will you just say that it's all right to not be spiritually aware?

For every situation there is almost always a choice to make.
One may seem right, one wrong, one hard, one for self's sake.
Will you choose the easy way and just drop out of the race,
or will you both do the right thing and finish the course with grace?

Might

Rich men dipped deep in their pockets and put in much.
The treasury increased in wealth through their Midas touch.
They were doing a good thing by sharing from their store,
But with their wealth they could have done much more.

Then one poor widow came and deposited her two meager mites.
She had seen many put in more and knew hers was very light.
But she also knew that she put in all that she had to give,
And that God would provide all that she needed to live.

Jesus sat quietly by and watched this touching scene unfold,
And knew it was a message for His own just waiting to be told.
He understood that pictures were a wonderful teaching tool,
And began to speak to help them drink from His learning pool.

See the wealthy men add their coins to the treasury coffer?
Do you see that the rich put in much and have _more_ to offer?
But notice that the poor widow deposits only mites—just two,
And I say she has put in more than all the rest—including you.

The rich do good to give to God much more than a mite,
But with their abundance they're not giving with all their might.
What the poor widow gave she did not offer in part.
It was ALL her livelihood, ALL her sacrifice, ALL her heart!

Mark 12:41-44

Hear My Prayer, O Lord

To me, O Lord, please grant Thy peace,
I pray that it will never cease.
How sweet Thy calmness in all life's storms.
I rest in peace in Your loving arms.

I cast my burdens at Thy feet,
And leave them there for You to treat.
What peace you give. You take my plight,
Your yoke is easy. Your path is light.

Through all my days, be Thou my Guide,
And stay with me right by my side.
I know that lost I'll never be,
For You are walking right by me.

Pray, give me right words when I speak,
To state Your truth and ne'er be weak.
What comfort that Your Word is true
And helps in all I say and do.

Lord, give me ears attuned to pain,
So others strength I may help regain.
O Lord, take charge in all my life,
So I can help others through their strife.

How pleasant is Thy healing touch
Which oft has strengthened me so much.
Thy health and blessings please bestow
On all Thy children here below.

The Parable of the Rich Fool

Luke 12:16-21

Then He spoke a parable to them, saying:

"The ground of a certain rich man yielded plentifully. And he thought within himself, saying, 'What shall I do, since I have no room to store my crops?' "So he said, 'I will do this: I will pull down my barns and build greater, and there I will store all my crops and my goods. 'And I will say to my soul, "Soul, you have many goods laid up for many years; take your ease; eat, drink and be merry."' "But God said to him, 'You fool! This night your soul will be required of you; then whose will those things be which you have provided?'"

"So is he who lays up treasure for himself, and is not rich toward God."

The Rich Fool

Luke 12:16-21

Some day, or night, your soul will be required of you,
But God has given you free choice as to what you may do.
All your life He has laid before you the path of death and life,
Helping you to choose by giving victory or guiding through strife.

I do not know how long the Lord will allow me to live.
I may have years on this earth or only a moment to give.
I am glad I've made my decision to give my life to Christ,
For then it does not matter how long I live or when I die.

I know that my eternal life began the moment I was born again,   John 3:16.17:3
That is when I repented of my sins and asked Jesus to live within.   Rom. 3:23
I am so glad that I will be with Jesus and that He will be with me,
And that we will be in Heaven with all other believers for eternity.

The other certain reality of which many people are unaware,
Is that there is another eternity opposite to Heaven up there.
Death is not an end-all, be-all, a moment when we cease to exist.
Hell is eternal: burning forever, a Lake of Fire, the Great Abyss!   Rev.20:10,14-15

If that scares you "to death", then good, it scares me, too,
And God may have to scare you with the knowledge of His truth.
It's because God loves ALL that He desires NO one should be lost,   Rom. 10:9-10
The death of Christ paid your entry into Heaven at the ultimate cost.

Jesus Is Always There

In my heart Jesus doth reside.
I am safe because He's by my side.
He's there in every circumstance of life,
Whether joy or sadness, gladness or strife.

His presence gives me peace and power,
As he guides me through each minute and hour.
His direction shows me the perfect way,
To live and love through all of the day.

His love keeps me stable and strong,
And gently helps me when I am wrong.
His discipline is swift, loving, and sure,
But given from His heart, perfect and pure.

His instruction shows me what is true and right,
As He teaches me lessons about His power and might.
His correction gently keeps me on the right path,
As the Good Shepherd guides me with His rod and staff.

In my heart, Jesus is always there.
His love and presence are beyond compare.
He is always there through all my strife,
Yearning to love and reach others through my life!

Inside Me

Jesus inside me is greater than he who is inside the world.
No matter what I come against He wins with His Word.
Jesus gives me His Spirit's sword to fight the enemy's attack.
It's the only weapon to use to keep satan off of my back.

Jesus teaches me His Word by His Spirit day by day.
As I read, study, and memorize it, I learn to use it His way.
Even Jesus did not use any other weapon when here on earth,
Though He is God's Son and knew how to use it from birth.

It is Christ in me which is the glorious hope that God made known.   Col. 1:27
If we have Christ, the seed has been in our heart miraculously sown.
God gives us His promise of His presence to teach us within,
His Spirit to guarantee us eternal life and freedom from sin.

Have you asked Jesus to come and live in your heart?
Are you willing to give Him all your life, not just part?
Have you experienced the freedom of Jesus inside?
If not, today is the day to begin letting Him reside!

From Before I Was Made

Psalm 139:13-18

For You, O Lord, have formed all of my parts inside,
And covered me in the womb where I did first reside.
I am fearfully, wonderfully made—all my praise to You I give.
Marvelous are Your works, my soul knows as long as I live.

I was made in secret in the lowest parts of the earth,
But my frame was not hidden from You before my birth.
Your eyes saw the substance of my unformed being,
In Your Book all my days were written before I began seeing.

How precious are your thoughts to me, O my God,   Psalm 139:17
Like glimmering jewels on the path that I trod.
If I could count them, how great the sum would be,
They would number more than the sands of the sea.

When I contemplate the magnitude of Your Truth to me revealed,
My mind is overcome with awe, my eyes opened, my spirit healed.
Quiet time in solitude with You is the most important thing I do,
For I am forever and always with the one who made me—You!

Tell-a-Vision

If you apply the Ten Commandments when watching TV,
How many programs do you think you should actually see?
You cannot say "It's only a show; this is not for real."
The image still enters your brain and leaves a lasting seal.

Everything that goes in must somehow come back out,
And leaves less room for you to be holy and devout.
So instead of having to clean up your act every day,
Turn off the TV and listen to what God has to say!

What God has to say trumps anything on any TV show.
He'll actually give you wisdom and help you His truth to know.
The more time you spend with God listening to His voice,
Means the time you turn on the TV will be less of a choice.

When a program comes on, ask "Which commandment does it break?",
Then watch only those shows which uplift and good character make.
Then all the extra time available from the shows you choose to ignore,
Use wisely to read God's Word, pray and spend time with your Lord.

Sweet Submission

Lord, gently and lovingly show me what is wrong,
But please don't do it without replacing it with song.
Handle me, change me carefully, for I can't do it myself,
I need Your gentle touch to change me into Your glorious wealth.

I think I understand that silence and submission is what You need,
Because I keep seeing how noisy and bossy I am and that I do not heed.
"Your relationship to your husband is a picture of your relationship to God"
Someone told me; so I'm in real trouble on the path that I currently trod.

I can't blame it on Eve's fall, genetics, environment, or on my parents role,
(just a little!) It's my fault, I think the world will fall apart if I'm not in
control.
It also doesn't work to be silent, calm, and composed on the outside,
When I'm arguing and erupting like Mt. Vesuvius on the inside.

I'm always analyzing, even now, judging and condemning <u>my</u> action,
But that just keeps me focused on the negative and losing traction.
So, please Lord, just change me now and put in a quiet, gentle spirit.
I know it is what You, John and I want, so I have faith You will do it!

(… and maybe deal with my impatience later!)

What Is It?

Prayer is sweet communion with my God,
He helps me on the path that I trod.
It's not just talk, my incessant chatter,
He lets me know that I really matter.

Prayer is praising God for who He is,
And always thanking Him that I am His.
Prayer is getting to know Him better,
Allowing Him to cut off every fetter.

Prayer is listening to His Words to me,
Being open to His love and wisdom totally.
Prayer is listening to His wise direction,
For I cannot lean on my own discretion.

Prayer is being open to His Holy Spirit,
Opening myself to His love without limit,
Confessing my sins so that I am free to grow
Into the unlimited love He wants me to know.

Jesus helps me even to know how to pray,
To stay close in touch with Him every day.
He teaches me how to praise and receive,
And is always with me to help me believe.

Blessings and Miracles

I'm nobody famous, not even one great,
I'm even anonymous to all those who rate.
But the miracles God has done for me are many,
And for you He'll do the same and give victory.

When you count your blessings, name them one by one,
That includes all the miracles for you that Jesus has done.
As you begin to list all of these wonderful things,
What wonderful memories of God's grace they bring.

You can't help but be lifted up in your present trial,
When recalling all of God's mercies bringing a sweet smile.
So lift high your head when storm waters rise,
Your God has saved you once; He will save you twice.

So count your blessings and your miracles, too,
You'll find that God has supplied many more than two.
That's because He sends you His grace, mercy, and love,
Through His only Son, Jesus, from Heaven above!

Miracles

In the middle of a barrage of sniper fire starting the Fiesta parade,
God saved me and my son with just one bullet to my leg.

A brown recluse spider bite certainly could have done me in,
But God had the only known antidote before nerves were ruined.

Depression so deep, no such thing as "tie a knot and hang on",
But God said "look up to Me and you'll be singing a song!"

Two nervous breakdowns, a plethora of ECT treatments, too,
God said "Do not worry, I will make you better than new."

As a single mom with very little means, a tree fell on my roof.
God sent a man to remove it; took in payment all the wood.

My son lost his only pair of glasses in a large rubber ball pit.
After we prayed, a little girl reached down and said "are these it?"

One Christmas Eve I succumbed to a lot of smoke I imbibed.
Doctor said "Basically you died", God said, "It's not your time."

So if you think that miracles stopped in Bible times,
Just take a look at a few of the miracles of mine.

God does His miracles each and every day,
Some "big" and some "small" each in their own way.

But if you really look at them from God's point of view,
Each miracle is something only God can plan and do.
The purpose, the timing, the grace, and mercy are only His,
So look at your life from His viewpoint and His miracles witness!

I've lost my physical, mental, emotional and financial health,
But with Jesus I've never lost my spiritual wealth.
He's given me back all I've lost and much more beside,
And I know that it's because He is Lord of my life!

Stroke Upon Stroke

John 21:25

Jesus left us all of His love and His legacy,
A perfect life and example for us to see.
He spoke volumes of words for us to hear,
Many written down by His followers dear.

But if all that Jesus did and the words He spoke
Were written down on paper, stroke upon stroke,
Not even the world could possibly contain
All the books that could be written in His name!

God Our Word-Giver

God is the Word-giver.
I'm only His Word-deliverer.
If I do not have His Words to spread,
My speech is as thin as gossamer thread.

He may give me words in my devotions daily
To read and share with souls so ready.
My own words would never touch or suffice,
Nor could I think of what to say; it might just sound nice.

Only God knows each one's hurt and heart.
Only God knows the right words to make a new start.
Only God knows what to say to start a hurt to mend.
Only God knows what and when His help to send.

God loves you enough to use whatever means He will,
To get His message to you and save you from ill.
He will use His Holy Word, your Pastor, a Godly friend,
Any way He can to let you know you are not forgotten.

He will speak the loving words that you need to hear.
You just need to be sure you have a listening ear.
He will guide and direct you on the path you should go.
Be ready because His path is the only one you need to know.

What is the Bible

How do I tell people who are bent on following their own ways,
And have no desire to search for You the rest of their days?
How do I let them know that Jesus is the ONLY path you approve,
That You love them and sent Jesus as the one way we're to move.?

I long to tell them that God's Word is like the air we breathe:
Daily inhalation is necessary for life, health, wisdom, enabling us to see.
First you need to know Jesus as your personal Savior and Lord,
Then He will help you as you read, to understand His Word.

The Holy Spirit will help you to read and understand
That His Word is your Daily Bread, your life, His plan.
Yes, it was written by many men separated by many years and places,
But guided by the Holy Spirit, they all wrote of God's great love and graces.

How would you feel if you came to your last day of living
Without ever having read His instructions on life, love and giving.
When we buy major items we read the enclosed "Instruction Book".
How much more should we read God's Word with an in-depth look!

It is a book, it is God's great source of truth, love and revival.
It is meant specifically to teach every one of us His method of survival.
You can never know the grand and glorious words of our awesome God,
Unless you read His Bible, our Life's Manual, to help us on the path we trod.

When to Read the Bible

If you're not a Christian, reading the Bible won't do much for you,
A veil covers your mind and the true meaning won't come through.   2 Cor. 3:14
Only after you accept Jesus as your Lord and Savior and pick up the Book,
Will the veil fall away as you read and study and you will get a clear look.

So many people "read" the Bible and say they just don't understand the text.
Some pick it apart, and ask "Why?" or "What for?" or "What follows next?"
The problem is not God, His Word, or the way it was written down for us.
The solution is in the relationship that the reader already has with Jesus.

It is in knowing Jesus that we have His Mind in studying His Word,
And in having Christ's Mind we learn to use His Spirit's Sword.
With the Spirit's help and tutorage, we can now study the Bible,
And we will be learning the only weapon effective against all rivals.

"All Scripture is God-breathed, for doctrine, reproof, correction,
instruction in righteousness that you may be on the way to perfection." Tim. 3:16
"These words which I command you this day shall be in your heart;
teach to your sons, talk as you sit, walk, lie down, rise up; do your part."   Deut. 6:6-7

"Every word of God is pure; if you trust Him He'll be your shield." Prov. 30:5
"You'll be blessed as you hear and keep His Word as Jesus revealed."   Luke 11:2
"Increasing your faith comes by hearing the Word of God.
Ask Jesus in your heart and journey with Him on the path you trod." Rom. 10:17

Your Gift

Here is the Word handed down to you as a Gift,
Given by the Father in love to teach and uplift.
The Word of Jesus leads you and inspires,
As the Holy Spirit guides to what your heart aspires.

The Word helps you grow in understanding His grace,
But it is the experience that makes you desire His Face.
His Book gives glimpses of His eternal joy and love,
But no other book can bring you love and joy from above.

Only God's Book can tell of His everlasting love for you.
He's written it all down in His Bible and gifted it, too.
When we receive a gift from someone we love above all,
We open it in great anticipation that we will be enthralled.

If we are then to put all our time and effort on the gift,
Ignoring the Giver, there would soon be between us a rift.
Our relationship would suffer and would cease to be as clear.
We would have the Gift but the Giver would not feel as near.

The Father, Yahweh, has given us His Gift, the Bible, His Word,
To teach, instruct, love, cherish, and guide; His own Spirit's Sword.
But He is the Giver, the Father, and the <u>Person</u> desiring your love.
Search the Word, but Jesus desires to give you His life from above.

His Abundant Life – John 10:10
His Eternal Life - John 3:16, 17:3
His Joy-Filled Life – John 17:13

Only God

Only God Seeds
Only God Feeds
Only God Grows
Only God Knows
Only God Begins
Only God Ends
Only God sees the Heart
Only God knows each part
Only God is the Master Teacher
Only God is our total Healer
Only God loves us heart and soul
Only God can make us His and whole
Only God could come down and become as men
Only God, as Jesus, could become our Friend
Only God loves us more than life itself
Only God wants us to love Him more than self
Only God has our perfect plan in mind
Only God desires for us to follow Him and find.

Springtime and Harvest

Thank you for the Winter and the trees so bare
Reminding us that You're in charge and You're there.
You take care of us during all seasons of our life,
And, there's a reason for each one, even cold, and strife.

We persevere and have faith through winter's cold,
Because of the firm hope that Spring's promise holds.
Of luscious grasses, colorful flowers and fresh rains,
And the smell of the earth coming to life again!

Summertime comes and warms the cold earth,
Encouraging the farmer's seed to give birth.
From many different seeds many crops will grow,
And the farmer sees God's miracle in every row.

As the Fall season approaches he reaps his harvest,
And gathers his precious bounty to take it to market.
He sells some to stores and some to farmers and friends.
He keeps some with thanksgiving and some he even lends.

Along with him we are all thankful for Your gracious providence
You offer as Your care in all the seasons every year as evidence.
We thank You that Your seasons are faithful, tried, and, true,
They come every year at their assigned time as sent by You.

All Lives Matter

Your life matters to our God.
He cares about every step you trod.
Whether the good things you do,
Or the bad that you go through.

God watches, forgives, cares and loves.
He desires that you set your sight on Him above.
He desires a relationship with you as if you're the only one,
Because He wants you to know Him, love Him, and Him alone.

You can know Him through His Son, Jesus.   John 14:6
He is the only One who came to save us.
When we believe in Him and His sacrifice on the Cross,
He forgives our sins and removes our dross.

We learn from His Word precepts and line upon line.   Isaiah 28:10
It is a growing, learning process that takes some time.
Just be patient because He wants you to finish the race,
And by looking in His Word to see His loving face.

Like the old children's song "Red and yellow, black and white,
They are all precious in His sight",
All lives matter to Him who created us to be
One family with Him for all eternity.

Your Life - Where?

I may be the only one in your circle of friends
To share with you how your life on earth ends.
Whether life eternal in hell or heaven above,
And the choice you need to make for the sake of love.

All humans have sinned in one way or another,
And have offended their God and their brother.
The penalty is death and there's only one way to pay,
God sent Jesus to die on the Cross, the only Way.

God loved us so much He was willing to let Jesus die   John 3:16
For all our sins, for all time, because of love, that's why!
He only asks that you respond, turn from your sins now,
Believe in His Son, and the sacrifice He made by His vow.

The beautiful thing about belief in the Lord Jesus Christ
Is that your Eternal Life starts then, not when you die.   John 5:24
You can begin to learn about Him as you read His Word,
He will teach you about Himself and His swift sword.

The more you study, the more of Himself He will reveal,
And poems, prayers, and promises and how you are sealed.
He will show you who you are (or were) without Him,
So you realize how blessed you are in Christ—sins forgiven--Forever!

John 3:16 "For God so loved the world, that he gave his only begotten Son, that whosoever believeth in him should not perish, but have everlasting life."

John 5:24 "Most assuredly, I say to you, he who hears My word and believes in Him who sent Me has everlasting life, and shall not come into judgment, but has passed from death into life."

It's You I Need

It's You I need Lord and more of You,
More of Your love, grace, mercy and Word so true.
But maybe it's for more of me that You pine:
More of my love, attention, prayers, and time.

God says: "You already have all of My love,
I was born on earth come down from above.
I lived among you and died on Calvary's tree,
To save you from your sins and make you free."

God says: "You already have all of Me",
"After all I died for you on Calvary's tree,
To show that no greater love has this among men,
Than to lay down one's life for one of his friends."

God says "I want you to live with Me eternally."
"I've made the only way for you to be with Me.
My Son, Jesus, is the way, the truth, and the life,   John 14:6
No one comes to the Father except by Jesus' sacrifice."

"So believe in My Son and never doubt My love.
It is sent to you especially from My throne room above.
If you want to feel closer to Me all you need to do is look,
Spend time every day in My love letter to you, My Holy Book!"

Trust in the Lord

Proverbs 3:5-7

Trust in the Lord with all your heart, vs. 5a
That means everything, not just a part.
You can trust Him with all your life,
When you know His plans are for good, not strife.

Lean not on your own understanding, vs. 5b
It is temporal, horizontal and fleeting.
God's wisdom is dispensed from up above.
He sees the end from the beginning, all in love.

In all your ways acknowledge Him, vs. 6a
So that your path will not grow dim.
God wants to know that in Him you believe,
So you are partners with Him whatever you achieve.

And he shall direct your paths, vs. 6b
You will not have to anticipate His wrath.
When you concede to doing things God's way
Your path will be bright and light as day.

Do not be wise in your own eyes, vs.7a
Remember that God's wisdom reaches to the skies.
We don't know or can plan what happens the rest of today.
God created us and knows us far better than we can say!

Trust the Lord

God says lean not on your understanding and trust Him with all your heart.
When something I'm going through is perplexing, the "why" is a big part.
But, even if I did understand, it would not help the situation, I find,
It would be my limited, narrow, horizontal thinking, my human mind.

My Father's thoughts are vertical and horizontal, much higher than mine.
I can only see limited. He can see everywhere, everyone, all the time.
His ways are higher than mine. He can make sure each person is educated.
His answers are always awesome, surprising, and perfectly orchestrated.

So instead of saying "I do not understand, why is this happening" in my life,
Say "I do not understand but I can trust You to get me through this strife.
I lean on Him in all my ways, good and bad, trust in His omnipotent hands,
Knowing that He has good for me and He will direct me in all my plans.

He is in charge of every person everywhere,
And will not let you be harmed, not a hair.
If you let Him direct every step that you take,
He promises to lead you for His Son's sake.

So trust Him with all your heart,
Over your own understanding quickly part.
Acknowledge Him in all your ways
And He shall direct you in all your days.

Proverbs 3:5-6

Proverbs 3:5-6

Create in me a clean heart, O God,
Make my life pure on the path that I trod.
I've tried and tried to do it on my own,
But there is no way I can do it, not alone.

You are the only one who can clean my heart,
Purify my mind, and give me a fresh start.
So I humbly bow before You for these three,
And pray that You grant them with Your rich mercy.

Everywhere I turn You give me Proverbs 3:5-6.
I've quoted it so much it really does stick.
"Trust in the Lord with all your heart";
The trusting is definitely my part.

"Lean not on your own understanding",
Don't trust it, mind, obey or even be trying.
"Acknowledge Him in all your ways",
Remember that means ALL your days.

"And He will direct you in all your paths",
Again He says, and means, ALL the ways you hath.
He knows, loves, and cares about all that pertains to you,
So lean on Him and He will see you through.

Two Choices

"There are only two choices that are important to make in this life,
One results in eternity in Heaven, one in eternal death and strife.
Unfortunately we have not been shown all that the Bible has taught,   Rev. 20:
All have eternal life, some in Heaven, some Hell as they ought!"   14-15

This choice happens to be one you can make for yourself,
When you confess your sins, believe in Jesus, ask for new health.
At this point you receive new birth and eternal life in Jesus Christ,   Jn. 3:16
Your salvation is assured, your name is written in His Book of Life.   Rev. 3:5

If you do not choose Jesus while you are alive on this earth,
You have already chosen to live where there will be no mirth.
Because No Choice means you have chosen against the Eternal King,
And decided to cast your lot in with satan and his fiery ring.   Mt. 25:46

If you choose anyone or anything but Jesus before you die,
The outcome is the same; that eternal location is where you'll reside.
If you happen to change your mind just before you go (expire),
Do it quickly because it is your last chance to escape the Lake of Fire.

Remember that your eternal life begins here as you ask Him in,   John 5:24
So why not start your life with the Father, Son, and Spirit and now begin.
He is waiting for you now and does not want you to perish forever,   2 Peter 3:9
But wants you to have Heavenly Eternal life that He will NEVER sever!

God's Armor

Ephesians 6:1-9

To be strong and able to proceed in God's power and might,
Put on His spiritual armor in order to be ready to win the fight.
Satan is strong and he will come against you like a giant,
But you can defeat him in the battle even though he is defiant.

Here is the armor that you need to put on every day:
Put on your waist the belt of God's truth protecting you in every way,
Next comes the breastplate of righteousness to lead you in a holy life,
Then shod your feet with the gospel and share it in peace or strife.

Above all take the shield of faith trusting in the Son,
You will be able to quench all the fiery darts of the evil one.
Put on the helmet of salvation to protect your mind and brain,
Use the Sword of the Spirit, the Word of God -- never refrain.

Remember the best way to wield the Spirit's sword
Is to stay immersed daily in God's Holy Word.
Read it in the morning when you first arise,
Repeat it, memorize it, and, keep it ever before your eyes.

Remember to pray unceasingly for all the Saints of God,
And expect them to pray for you on the path you trod.
Put on God's armor when you rise every single day,
And you will be ready for whatever comes your way.

Joy

True joy is not an emotion you dig up from inside,
It is a gift from God when in His faith you reside.
It doesn't work to pretend to be joy full when you're sad,
True JOY is to know Jesus, your friend, in good times and bad.

Have you ever tried to be joyful when it's just not there?
The JOY of Jesus goes deeper than imaginable than our care.
We try to find joy in people, things, activities, the human race,
But Jesus gives us JOY in His overcoming sins and His grace.

We try to find salvation in drugs, alcohol, sinful habits and ways.
Jesus gives salvation and JOY over all our sins for all our days.
We try to fill the emptiness with so many things in our "God-hole",
That God put there to fill with Himself and with JOY in our soul.

When we reach the end of ourselves and joy that we still cannot find.
Remember to search for Jesus, His Love and JOY are not far behind.
Remember that when even one person comes to faith in Christ the King,
That for JOY another one is saved, even all the angels together sing.

JOY is in the list that the Holy Spirit gives when one believes in the Lord.
Claim it as yours, let it fill you up as you read and grow in His Holy Word.
It is God who fills you with all JOY and PEACE when you hope and believe,
So you may abound in JOY, not by your flesh, but by His Spirit's power to receive!

Gal 5:22 But the fruit of the Spirit is love, joy, peace, longsuffering, kindness, goodness, faithfulness,

Rom 15:13 Now may the God of hope fill you with all joy and peace in believing, that you may abound in hope by the power of the Holy Spirit.

Grace

G od's infinite, overflowing love, and compassion to the human race
is what we call His amazing, unsurpassing, miraculous grace.
When we are called to be Your children we receive this gift,
to encourage us, free us, help us and our spirits uplift.

R eceiving His Grace given full and free
is the gift that He desires for you and me.
A Gift freely given from the Father has no strings attached.
It is given in love from His heart overflowing and unmatched!

A lways He is seeking those upon which to lavish His love,
especially to those who accept His Son, Jesus, now above.
He gives His special grace to all those who express faith
in His Son, for His sacrifice, to give them an eternal place.

C onsider now if it's even possible to entertain the thought
of the majesty, the beauty, the glory, and the Gift's cost.
The cost of the Gift is always to the Giver but to me it's free,
but do I stop to think of, or thank Him, or open it for me?

E very good and perfect gift comes from the Father above.
Isn't that a great definition of GRACE from our Father of Love?
The Father sent His Only Son, Jesus, to die on the Cross,
to give us the free Gift of Eternal Life and remove our dross!

Your Touch

You touch me with Your beautiful love,
And shower it like rain from above.
You touch me with Your overflowing grace.
How can I not in thankfulness seek your face.

You touch me with Your healing power.
Unending compassion is Yours hour by hour.
Your touch was the only one to heal the blind from birth.
There's nothing Your touch cannot heal on Your earth.

You touch me with friendship unsurpassing,
A friendship which will be eternally lasting.
You touch my heart with Your emotions you share.
I'm so glad You're my best friend and companion rare.

You touch me with Your desire to teach me all things.
What joy to my heart and wisdom this brings.
You are my supreme example whether life is up or down,
And Your touch makes my whole heart with love resound.

You know when I need the touch of Your Holy Spirit,
And You offer it to me in love without limit.
I am safe in Your loving arms enjoying Your love and care.
Your loving care insures to me that You will always be there!

God's Bottle of Tears

Psalm 56:8

Your Father loves you so much and cares for your sorrow and woe,
That He captures every tear of yours in His bottle just to let you know
That you are very special to Him and He cares about your sorrow.
So lean into Him -- cry those tears to One who cares about your tomorrow.

But there are more than tears of sorrow and woe in God's vial for you.
Haven't you ever cried tears of joy and happiness when you weren't blue?
Maybe at the birth of a baby, the closeness of a friend, family dinners,
Funny jokes, childrens' cavorting, pets' antics, and celebrating winners.

The tears in your bottle don't have to be all sad ones from your birth.
We know that Jesus laughed and wept when he walked on this earth.   John 11:35
Actually, both are a gift from the Father above to help us express
Our feelings, emotions, and share them with others to relieve our stress.

If He created tears for us to cry and a place in which to store,
Then He probably had reason to experience them even more.
Since Jesus wept over Lazarus His friend and Jerusalem His town,
It makes sense that our Father weeps over things that get us down.

There was the murder of all 2-year-olds by crazy Herod's scheme. Matt. 2:16
That would make any Father cry at the horrific sight of that scene.
Jesus' crucifixion was so horrid to the Father that He probably wept Matt.27:45
As He had to hide His face for three hours as darkness crept. Matt.27:46

But we know that the Father has much joy from His throne above
When He sees His children serving one another in joy and love.
When He and His angels see even one more accept Jesus as King Luke 15:10
They will rejoice, maybe with tears of joy, and certainly will sing!

Beautiful

B ecause of Jesus' love for me
E ventually in Heaven I'll be,
A ll the days planned ahead
U nder the guidance of our loving Head.
T his is the citizenship of my legal birth,
I 'm only a visitor to this alien earth.
F or now I work, laugh, live and play
U ntil Jesus comes to get me on that date,
L eaving earth for eternity; I can't wait!

Relationship

There is nothing more important in Heaven or Earth,
not in its length nor in its wide, wide girth,
Than my relationship with my Savior Jesus Christ.
He is my best Friend, my all, my very life.

It started when I was 12, when He gave me new birth,
And the knowledge I gain from Him is of infinite worth.
I study His Word daily with His Spirit by my side.
He's a loving, wise, all-knowing, Teacher, and Guide.

His Word cuts sharper than between marrow and bone.   Heb. 4:12
He uses it to rout out sin to which I'm so prone.
Then He puts in His Word of love and so many things.
I am filled with peace, love, joy, and my heart sings.

"Study to show yourself approved" says He.   2 Tim. 2:15
It is a blessing and privilege to keep that habit daily.
His Word is living and powerful and I feel Him near
As He reveals Himself deeper, closer, and more dear.

You may read a verse meaning something one time
And read it later and the Spirit brings it really alive.
After all, Jesus is "the Way, the Truth and the Life".   John 14:6
His Word is living and powerful to you who abide.

It Can Only Be Jesus

After Jesus' arrival was met with joy at His miraculous birth,
By Mary, Joseph, shepherds, and wise men bringing myrrh.
A very sad, horrendous slaughter of all boys under age two
Occurred when mad Herod tried to get rid of Jesus, too.

Joseph had a dream in which an Angel spoke:
"Take the boy and his Mother to Egypt", then he woke.
So he took his family to Egypt and there they did hide,
Until Herod finished his terrible murderous reign and died.

Again the Angel spoke and said it was okay to go home.
Joseph could go back to Israel by the way they had come.
But he was afraid of Archelaus in Judea, Herod's son,
So they settled in Nazareth of Galilee fulfilling what's told.

All this to say you can see how God protected His only Son,
The circumstances that there was only one Messiah, only One.
Have you ever thought that Jesus was the only person alive,
Who could fulfill the conditions and age that He was at that time!

Just think, there was <u>no</u> other person in all of the land of Israel
Who could answer all of the prophecies and all He could fulfill.
But this prophecy was especially one that Herod brought true:
There were <u>no</u> boys left in the land except Jesus under age two!

Matthew 2:16-23

The Anointing of Jesus

The Spirit of the Lord God was upon Jesus Christ our Lord.
The Father anointed Jesus and into His Spirit He fully poured.
Preach the good tidings to the poor; and the brokenhearted heal,
Proclaim liberty to captives, the prisoners bound, open their seal.

The acceptable year of the Lord freely proclaim,
Also the day of vengeance of our God do the same.
In the land of Zion comfort and console all who mourn,
Give beauty for ashes, for mourning the oil of joy adorn.

The garment of praise for the spirit of heaviness,
So they may be called the Lord's trees of righteousness.
God clothes the Son and He is with joy greatly filled.
With salvation's garments, righteousness' robe, He is thrilled.

As the earth brings forth its bud and flower,
The garden causes things to grow by His power.
So the Lord will cause righteousness and praise
To spring forth by the Son and by His grace.

So we see by the Father's prophecy and loving hand,
All the ways He gave to Jesus for control over the land.
By loving the poor, healing the sick, freeing those in jail,
We knew He would be a kind, loving Messiah, from Israel!

Isaiah 61:1-11

What's My Name?

When someone introduces you by name at a gathering at night,
Doesn't it feel good when everyone who attends gets it right?
Nothing feels worse than having your name mispronounced,
Called wrong, you're embarrassed, want it correctly announced.

Now since we as mere mortals can feel this about our personal label,
Think how God feels when we misuse His name, His special Title.
We call our Creator: God, Father, Jehovah, Jesus, more beside,
But, "J", was not created until more than 1400 years after Jesus died.

God has made it clear that His Name is, will always be, YAHWEH,
And, is in His Son's Name, YAHSHUA, the Savior and only Way.
Search your Scripture and you will most certainly find contained,
Our Father in Heaven desires to be called by the name <u>He</u> ordained.

So next time someone mispronounces or calls you by the wrong name,
Remember how offended and hurt you are to be excluded by the same.
Realize that our Father also has given us His Special Name to call Him by,
And we are privileged to be allowed to address Him directly by it anytime.

He loves for His children to call Him by name the right way,
That means knowing His correct name and using it – YAHWEH.
Maybe our Father would hear and answer prayers given in His Name,
If we were more careful to pray, worship and praise as He has ordained.

Which Way to Go

Don't look to your <u>left</u> where all the liberals and naysayers are.
If you listen to them you'll be depressed that they want to war.
Don't look to your <u>right</u> even though it may seem better to you.
Sometimes their opinions agree and sometimes they're very few.

Now it's certainly not going to help to look <u>down,</u>
Getting depressed at everything that's going <u>around.</u>
The only way you can keep your head above the fray,
Is to <u>look up</u> and keep asking God to show you the way!

For anyone the job you hold is quite an impossible task,
Doing the best you can and making decisions that last.
Remember to keep looking up and asking advice from God.
He's the only Counselor you can trust on this daily path you trod.

Instead of looking in all directions that can upset and confuse,
Make prayer in His direction your first priority, your first weapon to use.
We will pray with you each day for God to be your first Guide,
And I'm sure as you <u>look up</u> you will see He's on your side.

The most important direction each day on which to focus before you go
Is to read God's Word so that you have His wisdom to fight every foe.
Using your time to know Him first thing before you start every day
Can unimaginably help you in a positive, wise, loving, and caring way!

Make America Great!

The only way we the people can make America great again
Is for God's people to look at themselves and confess their sins.
Then in 2 Chronicle 7:14 we are to humble ourselves, pray,
And seek God's face as we turn from our wicked sinful way.

Then when we go through this necessary process on our part,
God makes some promises from which He will not depart.
He says He will hear our prayers from His heavenly throne:
He'll forgive our sins, heal our nation, and we'll not be alone.

Remember a nation divided cannot stand for the good of all.
By definition there are at least two factions headed for a fall,
But that division will always bring the whole nation down.
People will wonder what happened to their state and town.

We need to stop fighting what we think is wrong on the other side,
And look at ourselves for things we can improve where we reside.
If we begin to work on things where we know we can assist,
We won't have as much time to attack and negatively persist.

God's Word plainly states that it begins with believers of God's race.
We must humble ourselves and pray and continually seek His face.
We must individually confess and turn from our own evil and sin,
So He will forgive, hear, and heal our America into greatness again!

2Ch 7:14 if My people who are called by My name will humble themselves,
and pray and seek My face, and turn from their wicked ways, then I will
hear from heaven, and will forgive their sin and heal their land.

I Would Like to Speak With You

I'm sitting here on My Throne waiting to spend time with you.
I have all the time until you're through with what you have to do.
I know you have work, chores, shopping, cooking, friends, too.
I'm willing to wait until you're ready to give me a minute or two.

You can hear My voice much clearer if you take a little break,
Grab My Word and read a few verses and then concentrate.
Clear your mind by spending a few minutes with Me alone.
The time in prayer will set your ears to just the right tone.

Do not be afraid of anything that I might have to say.
As my precious child, I always speak to you in love this way.
You may wonder why you have never listened closely before,
Because this is the key that opens our relationship's door.

Now you're ready – just say "Lord I'm ready to hear,
Speak to me the message you want me to hold dear.
Tell me what You would have for me to say or do today,
Please speak the word and with Your help, I will obey."

It humbles me greatly that You desire to speak to me,
and that You desire to listen to me when I pray to Thee.
The fact that You hear and answer Your children here below,
Is a picture of our beautiful relationship that can grow and grow!

God's Fellow Workers

Still a Babe in Christ, having to be milk-fed, is this you? I Corinthians 3:1-9
Or is the solid food of His Word what you like to chew?
Do you say I'm "Baptist, Methodist, Lutheran" even for His sake,
Then the following is a "carnality" test just for you to take.

Do you say you belong to a certain sect like those above?
Yes? These are but groups through which you learn God's love.
Is your heart sometimes filled with envy, strife and division?
Yes? Then you're behaving carnally—like mortals without vision.

The Lord gives to each one according to his gift:
One may sow, one may preach, one my water, one uplift,
But none of these is anything to be followed or adored,
Because all of the increase comes directly from the Lord!

God hates divisions, sects and all of the resultant strife.
He has given us <u>oneness</u> in Christ and an abundant life.
We are God's fellow workers, building the house, sowing the field,
And we will each of us receive our reward according to our yield.

If you have never accepted Jesus Christ as your Lord and Savior and received His guarantee of eternal life, recognize your position as a sinner (Romans 3:23--"for all have sinned and fall short of the glory of God"), repent of your sins and believe in Jesus and ask Him to come into your heart today (Romans 10:9-10--that if you confess with your mouth the Lord Jesus and believe in your heart that God has raised Him from the dead, you will be saved!) And, my favorite verse where Jesus says in John 5:24 --"Most assuredly, I say to you, he who hears My word and believes in Him who sent Me <u>has everlasting life</u> and shall not come into judgment, but <u>has passed from death into life</u>." (Emphasis mine) Begin your personal relationship with Jesus today!

Your fellow Christian, Sharon

Printed in the United States
By Bookmasters